VARIATIONS
ON A THEME

Selected Poems
by
Mother Mary Francis, P.C.C.

VARIATIONS on a THEME

by Mother M. Francis, P.C.C.

FRANCISCAN HERALD PRESS
Chicago, Illinois 60609

Variations on a Theme by Mother Mary Francis, P.C.C., copyright © 1977 by Franciscan Herald Press. All reprint permissions of poetry or art reserved to the publisher.

Library of Congress Cataloging in Publication Data:

Mary Francis, Mother, 1921-
    Variations on a theme.

    1.   Christian poetry, American. I. Title.
PS3563.A745V3   811'.5'4   77-1971
ISBN 0-8199-0664-6

to
Right Reverend Alan C. Clark,
Bishop of East Anglia
minstrel of the Lord

Author's Note

A sequel to WHERE CAIUS IS, poems of earlier years, this selection is made from poems of riper years with the exception of *A Song for April* which was written when I was a postulant.

—Mother Mary Francis, P.C.C.

CONTENTS

I.
DAYS OF
OUR LIFE

VARIATIONS ON A THEME

"For I claim that love is built to last forever."
—psalm 89

I. *Persevering water*
roading the waste of rock
with delicate domination, trickling tons
of granite to forever-ed passways,
love is.

II. *Built to outlast the window is the cheek*
pressed hard against it.
Eye outlives the road
it watches for reward of tears that
love is.

III. *Forever smiles the flower at the wind*
gusting it into death
of perfume rising
from shredded petals' triumph when the wind all
spent is.

IV. *Long sprawls the sphinx*
in pyramids to dust doomed.
Point of the frail desire of spirit turns
straight onto Love that summons piercing, drenching
with ever-and-forever tide the little
pyramided day-on-day thing
love is.

3

A SONG FOR APRIL

April, my April,
Mine! for young
Are you as my heart and its hopes are young.
Spilling the balm of your tears to bless
My own with its fragrant tenderness,
April, my April,
You are as young
As my undreamed dreams, my songs unsung.

April, shy April,
Yet be not shy
With me who love you. Your hand in my
Own hand, we two shall race the dawn,
Your fleet white feet and mine upon
Its clouds, till all
The must of care
Grows sweet in the scent of your tangled hair.

April, glad April!
And how be sad,
My heart? The earth is young! And clad
In tender laughter are older woes.
On every road my April goes
She breathes her laughter
In cinnamon dreams
And folds it in polished shoots of green.

My wilful April,
        You hide your charms
From dreamless hearts. Your slender arms
Have no embrace for those whose eyes
Can see no vision in the skies.
        And them who fear
        To weep, you scorn,
For your sweet laughter of tears was born.

April, gay April!
        Will you ever be gay
And curve of your lips be rose always?
Let May unflower, let June grow old,
But April about her gaily folds
        Her verdant mantle,
        The silver cord,
And dances back to springtime's Lord.

INVOCATION OF THE HOLY SPIRIT UPON A BRIDE AND GROOM

Come, Spirit,
Holy Spirit,
In bright brooding on this mystery
Mystic with love
That springs full-limbed from You.

Be to this girl
The graces of her hands,
Hallow the raptures rippling down her joy.

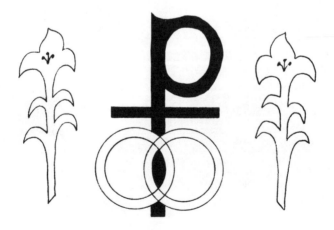

Be for the darkling future,
Quenchless Blaze.
Sit on her chaste heart
Ever-jealous Flame!
Come to the upper chamber of her soul
Consecrate, inviolate for this day.
Be of her love the splendid Aureole,
Of her faith, the whitely blazing Crown!

Come, Gift,
Be given newly to this man.
Love of the Son and Father,
Now descend on his kept heart
And be of his resolve
The strength eternal,
Be upon his vows
The Seal wild, wheeling worlds
Can never melt.

Be now best Gift and Comforter,
The Pledge of his white troth
And of his hope, the End!

Come, Spirit,
Holy Spirit,
In bright brooding on this mystery,
To this man, a Pentecostal vow,
To this girl, a Kiss upon her brow.

PSALM 116

Appoint some seraph to proclaim
Reasons for praise,
To breathe out documental flames
Concerning Essence and Priority.

Angelic choruses will make the theme
Endless polyphony:
"Praise Might, praise Majesty!" Alone, the heart
Listens in vain to catch its alto there.

Better to spell such praises as I know:
Green mercy pushing
With tireless patience through resisting clods
Of pride polite with frost;

Wiser to sing God's awful perseverance,
Invent new modes
To bear the music of His sleuthing pity
Fast on the slender clue of a secret sigh.

His truth remains forever, underscoring
The sophistries in all my best excuses.
Try to outrun His mercy! Seek to baffle
The logic of His Love, and at the end

Fall, panting, straight into His grave compassion,
Drop in the saving snare of truth. All nations,
Come! Praise the walls and rooftops of His pity,
Sing His truth as fatal as salvation.

WASHDAY

Army set in array,
The white guimpes hang there,
Rack upon rack,
And quieting steam of breath
Before a new fresh forage into God's
Mysteries.

Disciple to their lore,
I ponder guimpes: the pure Communion cloth
At dawn, the white drapes on the lifting breasts
Kept secret for the King.

I study tents
That shelter fragile dreams with peach perfume
Essenced from morning's sculleried Song of Songs,
And know the battlesmoke of daily war
With Powers and with Principalities.

Flags of identity,
The white guimpes wave there,
Rack upon rack.
I pledge allegiance to
A Lover.

Let the totalled world come hear it:
My Lover is mine, and I am His hard-won
Victory over the dark and all confusion.
And guimpes to tell it!

                    Then the racks
Heave up their innocent burden till I see
My sisters faithfully raising, faithfully setting
The guimpes with given heartbeats.

                         Quick, I turn
Away, for secreting the sudden tears.

HOLY THURSDAY

It was the dust storm did it,
Coated halls
With fragiler-than-clay beds for imprinting
Footprints for Eucharistic meditation.

Sisterhood is written
In the toes
Lapping and overlapping in the dust.
Bare feet going and bare feet returning.

I gaze in tenderness upon the blurred
Print of someone stopped to ponder, rubbing
The silky dust into memorial.

But then I stop to smile down
At the firm print
Of messenger on errand. "Work to do!"
Is written in the dust. I shall remember.

And when determined novice comes with mop
Hungry for dust, to wipe away my musing,
I shall forgive her, having Eucharistic
Meditation dusted-fine on heart.

SUMMER SEMINAR

Up from my knees and coiled with good resolve,
I lightning-ed on the garden, striking east
And west from thunders of the heart's desires.

Never was there beginning till this day!
Never again would love lag, song run down!
Two hundred sparrows all remarked: Amen.

When the trees shook their tambourines, I smiled
Gracious acknowledgement to every leaf.
Oh, good to see creation so informed
Of transformation, utter, ultimate!
With benign toes I gently smoothed the moss
Where under dusty dome the turtle dreamed.

Sensing I had a message, he looked out,
Prodigal with patience, having no
Luncheon engagements and adverse to speed.
I mentioned how the world had just been made
This morning, and he rolled with seldom-used
Invisible cord, thick shutters up from eyes.

(Sienna? Chestnut? Crimson splashed on brown?
How can I tell you of the turtle's eyes?)
With sudden insecurity, I read
To him the cast of characters for fear
He'd think that the philosopher was he,
And told him, with a few affectionate taps
Upon his dome, that life was clear to me.

Further the turtle's head thrust out, the neck
Losing its crepe with reaching. Who could know
A turtle's head might look so far? One claw
Showing bright red mosaics turned toward me
So like a helping hand that I became
Large and ridiculous in the moss. Less sure,
I told again my wisdom to the turtle,
Rehearsed for him my newfound clarities.

Slowly the long neck turned its lollipop head
East by northeast above the moss. Just then
Sun rivetted diamond tears in the old eyes.

Shaken and unprepared, I crouched, abashed
There in the moss, before the turtle's gaze.
(What does one say before a turtle's tears?)
But shining with ageless wisdom, wet brown rings
Shuttered themselves, all commentary made;
Head under dome retreated, claw closed in.
And so the interview ended.

                                All unsprung
Before the wonders of Your ways, I know,
Lord, of Your gifts this was not least, this one,
Tutoring certainties to contingency
Of me on You.

            What else can I resolve?
I will remember the tear in the turtle's eye.

DETAILS FOR THE DEATH OF OUR LADY

Give her now for this brief hour
Into the chivalrous arms of darkness.
Lay her upon the bosom of the earth,
Gently, a grain of wheat again
That gave us Bread before.

Snuff for a tender moment the flame,
The dull earth's single splendor. Heaven, bend
A hushed, expectant arc across her grave.
Patrol on wings of flame, you Seraphim,
This place of the buried wheat!

Let the trees kneel, apostles at her grave;
Apostles stand like trees and wait the sign
For springing, sprouting, blossoming. Now, world,
Be mausoleum for one tender sheaf
This hour of your best glory!

Planted by us, watered with God's desire,
Sleep in our earthy hostel, Mary. Swiftly
Comes His increase for you, His briefest dead.
Back, stand back, you Seraphim!
The gallant earth is heaving
A glorious reluctance for her sprouting!

Down to the southland of her grave
On bright propellors, spread your brave formations,
Birds of the earth she loved, and strike the moment
Of rising with your thousand throaty chimes.
Never again alone, small grain of wheat,

Spring, sprout, and blossom, spread your fruits across
The floors of Heaven. Be a Queen forever.
Only remember you are ours and walked
Under our trees and slept, once, in our earth.

HOSPITAL ROOM, MID-SUMMER

Yes, now I understand
Why You have judged
It absolutely urgent I should be
Here, on this bed.

Someone must watch that tree
Hurt with the heat but unfrustrate for grace
Limpen and lean to seek a secret breeze
Small as my sigh
For swaying burnt leaves down
And up in piteous, perfect dance
Of faith.

One day a wantoning wind
Will win again
Exuberant ensemble from those boughs
Ravished by spring.

You call it essential now,
This hour thick with summer's personal doom,
That someone watch the tree refuse to be
Unbeautiful.
Yes, Lord, I understand
My work, and do it gladly.
Only, please,

Spare me the need to cease my work to reach
Out for the hospital kleenex. Cup Your hand
On my, amen! and catch

RETREAT MEDITATION

"The fear of the Lord is the beginning of Wisdom."

first prelude:
Yahweh, I heard your anger snap the day
In two. I saw your wrath
Smoke out the sun.
Bats of my sins were tangled
In my hair
There where I died of fear

(And heard a loved Voice say:
"Daughter, arise!").

Oh! these distractions!
Start again now with the

second prelude:
After the body's failing, His the right
To hurl that soul-filled van
Into the pit.
Picture the flames till trembling
Melts your knees,
Dismantles your spine with fear

Of Him (whose Cross tilts down
One inch from hell).

resolution:
Your love unravels my best-knitted fears.
Your mercy sceptres every smiting rod.
Forgive my thoughts that cannot think of swords
Except to see a lance-wound on a Heart.

the final sweet despair:
Of wisdom, fear is the beginning. True.
But, Lord, is there perhaps some other way?

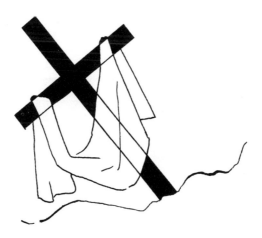

SCALES

Piano: for Beginners.
And I, ten,
With destiny declared: brain surgeon, I.
(And yes, of course, the greatest in the world.)
This was an insult. For beginners played
About a robin in a cherry tree
Who would sing a pretty song to me.

Still, with my tongue trapped
In determined teeth,
I doggedly invoked the robin. Straight
And stiff-perched on piano bench, I begged
Of lifeless bird up in that painted tree,
For duty's sake, a pretty song to me.

Concertos are for later.
Play the scales
Over and again (that cherry tree!).
There will be tumultuous rhapsodies.
(Remember your grandfather, dear.) The opus
For little girls concerns a bird and tree
And how there comes a pretty song to me.

Older than ten, symphonic movements drop
Inadequate for me. I turn back now
From rhapsodies and seek once more the scales,
Tapping the first small tune of love again,
Found now the only adequate, the call
Beat out again and over in the heart:
O Lover, from your stark and blood-ripe Tree,
Sing your persistent song of love to me.

OCTOBER WEDDING ANNIVERSARY

When the martyring wheel of season
Dismembers the summer
To gold-crisp, death exhales
Her cinnamon plumes
Of air for festival. What mourner dares
Debauch with grief this bright, exultant dying!

So do You come,
Unhinging my springs and summers,
Flinging the heart-gates wide
For quickening death.

Autumn-tutored, I strew
My leaves of being
Across Your breast, my Lover,
While my songs
Rehearse the cadence of a woman loved.

CONCERNING HOSPITALITY

Because You are a most distinguished Guest,
I offer You my best accommodations:
My tent of skin pitched carefully on these
Supporting limbs. You will admire the view
Of sky and earth available through these
Two casements of my eyes. But if the light
Of Your bright outer craft makes too-fierce noon,
Notice the parchment blinds of eyelids, draw them
By fringing lashes down, and rest a while.

For Your consideration, let me line my thoughts
On avenues of brain all neatly laid
For Your convenience when You stroll my mind
On Your investigations in the evening.
For morning walks, there is my soul to stride.
Then, may I venture to suggest, for dreaming
In cool repose: the meadows of my breast?
At Your disposal, acres of my being,
Triune God. Do please feel quite at home.

I am aware You are a Lover, wanting
Attentive hearing and the proper score
Of background music for Your ceaseless courting
Of me against outside flirtations. Only
Dial my heart to largo or to presto
As You prefer, to symphony or hum.
You do remember surely how to turn it
Off completely when You wish? You merely
Look one single moment longer at me.

THE MENDING

There is no shattering love cannot mend,
No shards its gentle hands shall not make whole.
Healing, its glances brush like wings across
The deepest rawness of the heart, and leave
At last, at last no trace of briney woe.

What though we walked in ruins of a dream,
What though our tears had faded out the rose
And gold of what was once a splendid bond?
There is no shattering love cannot mend,
No shards its gentle hands shall not make whole.

Sweet is the love that never knew a wound,
But deeper that which died and rose again.

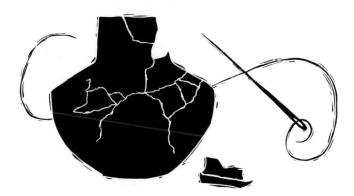

TRYST

I shall be there, I promise!
Just when the thought strikes half-past weary.
There shall I wait, my Darling,
Under my swaying cherry tree of heart.
Remember the day You carved Your initials in it?

Shall I wear hope? You always
Tell me I look loveliest in that.
Faith-flowers in my hair? Yes, surely!
I know Your taste, but tell me once again!

We shall sing my unsung songs together,
Till vines reach up around us, thinking we
Are part of some forever. I'll be there,
I promise You, when love chimes quarter-past yearning

And look to see You running down the groves
Of my desire on feet that summon flowers
From an unlikeliest sod. I shall be there
Tilted at my life's edge, until You come.

II.
VOCATION

QUEEN OF
CRAFTSMEN

Blow by exquisite blow,
The crystal hammers of her love
Fasten the careful joinings of His bones.
Prophets have sung this craft: how men may number
These bones, but never break an one of them.

What blueprint guides you, Queen of architects,
To trace sure paths for wandering veins
That run Redemption's wine?

Who dipped your brush, young artist, so to tint
The eyes and lips of God? Where did you learn
To spin such silk of hair, and expertly
Pull sinew, wind this Heart to tick our mercy?

Thrones, Powers fall down, worshipping your craft
Whom we, for want of better word, shall call
Most beautiful of all the sons of men.

Worker in motherhood, take our splintery songs
Who witness What you make, in litanies:
Oh, Queen of craftsmen, pray for us who wait.

PSALM FOR
A DOCTOR

Bless Thou my hands with gentleness,
My eyes with healing glances,
The while I seek Thy mysteries
In tent of flesh, on jagged cliff of bone.

Let me discover Thy inventive Love
Whether it lurk in cage of rib,
Pulse in the motored heart, or lie
Subtly shuttered by the silk of eyelid.

Let me walk humbly, God, these avenues
Of Thy high artistry and handiwork.
Mine not to work in steel, to carve in wood,
To paint with oils, but mine to enter in
This human sanctum of Thy best creation
And find Thy image and Thy likeness there.

God of Wisdom, radar my decisions,
God of Power, shape my hands to heal.
God of Mercy, let Thy pity stream
Out of me on every human pain.
                              Amen.   Amen.

PSALM FOR AN ARCHITECT

God whose fingers taper mountains,
Who summons trees, whose comments are
Lightning down the skies, whose laughter
Spirals silver in all fountains.

Grant that I may always be
Driven by a dream of Thee.

Goaded, questing, let me wander
The earth to wring its beauties free,
Fling up walls to tell Thy power,
Roofs to speak Thy love's stout shelter.

Grant that I may never be
A man at rest, but seeking Thee.

That I may build, God, lay in me
Thy granite Wisdom's own foundations.
Etch Thy Beauty on my spirit,
Thy blueprints trace each day in me.

Creator-God, this may I be:
One flinty spark, but struck off Thee.

DIALOGUE

I am glad I thought of philosophers,
God said.
Their strenuous efforts swear in public confession
How my thoughts are not the thoughts of men.

Engineers to pan all stuff of earth
Are good
For witness of my ways' meandering
With casual mirth the sweat of all invention.

Artists to keep my archives in good
Order,
Poets to epic major enterprises
Of mine, spread out my glory everlasting.

The whole arrangement I have made,
God said,
Has worth. I like that race of theologians
Turning my diamond, face by face, on men.

Only I wish someone would chance
Along
To marvel at a candle through a window,
Slosh bare-ankled in the dew, and laugh

Because my ballerina gnats annoy
Some larger, graver creatures.
No one saw, I fear, (God said)
The mint blade in the gravel.

I know men are so busy telling
The story of me (even if unknowing).
I shall not regret the captains, thinkers,
Doers, talkers, workers,
Even makers. I only wish
(God said)
There could be someone now to notice things
I do just for your pleasure.

And I said:
Lord, take me!

AUTOBIOGRAPHY

Part I:
   While swallows dipped through my heart,
   I tilted handfuls of sunlight over my hems:
   Braid of fantastic gold. I told the doves
   Poised on my shoulder: to be loved is to be lovely!

   I sat and awaited Him,
   Songs chasing down my veins;
   Sat and awaited my death,
   My skirts like waterfalls around me,
   Morning in my hair
   And all my bracelets waking
   Into flowers,

                    Until He came. The low knock,
   Oh, the moment! I did not sing. I was song.
   The song was: Lover, Lover, it is I!

   But the latch was not lifted. The footsteps
   Drifted back like a sigh.

Part II:

A raven sits on my heart,
Listens to winds cry at the marrow of me.
My fingers stroke the unreality
Of air on which my lonely vigil feeds.

I kneel and await Him,
Tears rutting all my songs,
Kneel and await my death,
And rue my skirts with climbing torn,
Night lapping at my ankles.

My bracelets pawned to buy me faith,
Deliberate destiny burns beneath
My eyelids. Listen, raven, listen!
All that I cannot understand, I know!

And this is the moment; fingers on the latch
Of me, He asks who dwells here. Hoarsely comes
The final whisper: Lover, it is Thou!

Latch lifts. Footfalls, footfalls,
He enters in.

WHOM GOD LOVES, HE CHASTISES

"Whom God loves, He chastises; and He
scourges every son whom He receives."
—Heb. 12, 6

Reciprocally suds-splashed, skirts colliding
In narrow cloisters, or invoking gravely
The Trinity's Third Person on
Our shelling of the peas,
We laced the communal months with strings of days
Lifted from shared profundities, together,
Investigated midnight with our psalms,
Summoned the dawn with antiphons, and pondered
With hymns the twilight mysteries, together,

Not braced for flat of hand on cheek of life,
On fragile pulse of heart, till sunlight was
Shadow-invaded, shade-infested, stricken
With sudden spectres.

                    Tilting soul on soul
Came God to write the great good news of love
Deeper, deeper in the cauterized hearts.

IN FEAR AND TREMBLING

"Serve the Lord with fear;
rejoice before Him in trembling."
—psalm 2

Because I fear
I might not hear
Your whispered: "Daughter,
Walk upon the water!"
I shall serve You, Lord,
In leaning on Your word.

And fear be all my grace.
My gaiety, Your face
Hid in remotest bliss
Penetrated by my kiss.

The high romance
Of hope's bright dance
Needs elevation
Past my station

Except by practised tremble
I find the vast ensemble
Of cosmic dance is grace
Shaken by Your face.

So shall I serve You, Lord,
Who laughed; and there was Word.

MISSIONARY

"The conversion of oneself is a much greater
thing than the conversion of many sinners."
　　　　—Father Leonard Foley, O.F.M.

From what difficult tundra
Have you come,
Young apostle, with your cunning captive?

From what unchartered regions,
Halting veteran,
Do you drag your solitary convert?

In jungled arteries and tropical veins
The battle rages,
Smoke of logic curls
Around the fragile walls of brain cell, choking
The thin defenses humming in the heart.

So you come home,
Home from the mission field no one shall find,
Home to small-talk of world annihilation
With shining wreckage of your own undoing
Strewn on the day.

　　　　　　　　I sing your conquest, knowing
What dark threats follow it!
Elusive convert,
Never quite tamed, I wonder
How many obscure baptisms you will need.

PSALM FOR THE RENEWAL OF VOWS

Antiphon: *Build no monument to the day it was done: ***
this is the day of its doing.

*Tell not of promises made: ***
strike now their moment of making.
*Creation is just now created ***
to witness an April awaking.
*See those ants crazily running ***
all ways at once to proclaim it!
*Sunflowers adding wild cubits ***
of height to look in where the flame sits
*All at once kindled in sun-dish ***
for lighting this day of the promise!
*Go, and discover the flowers ***
vesting in color, for from this
*Moment is measured forever ***
all my forever-and-evers;
*Backward and forward, and never ***
quite thought of before Lord. Amen.

Antiphon: *Build no monument to the day it was done: ***
this is the day of its doing.

KING'S COUNCIL

From the four zones of my universe
They come, the rulers of my dioceses:
Fine-featured dreams and hawk-nosed fears,
Shabby compromises with scrawny necks.

Ageing hopes pull back their rounding shoulders.
Love comes in borrowed crimson, having spent
Her robes on the unbeautiful. And, last
That patriarch, old faith, comes shuffling in.

Here is the council of me, God. Look! see,
Them all cast down their mitres at your feet!

III.
FRANCIS
AND
CLARE

NO MYTH FOR CLARE

Because you are light,
I looked for a haze of dawn
Pearling my sorrows over,
Kept careful vigil
For warmth and wonder
To scatter persistent night.

Only you came,
No spatter of dawn on sky,
But pitiless light
To show the rose's thorns,
Beacon to point
The bramble on the way.

Break on my heart, then,
Your fantastic light!
Clean with your flame the dinginess unfit
For light to look on.

What droll masquerade
Has made you, woman of light, a tender myth
On tapestry pale-lovely and remote?
No! I will shout your true identity.
Unmask you to the world, sweet lady of light,
Of light that rescues soul from shadow's comfort,
Of light plunged, swordwise, deep into the heart.

EPITAPH

Here lies the ideals of Saint Francis:
Pressed in the folds of earth, the little plant,
Drooped to a smile of meager flesh and bone.

Here lies the triumph of the little poor man:
The lovely, wasted witness to his dream.
Bring no polite compassion to her coffin
And stay the pitying upward flight of brow
For Francis and his dream without a haven,
His mad, impossible schemes. Here lies the proof
His dream was wholly possible to her heart.

Here lies the refutation for crawling cautions;
Sweet, mute rebuttal to any compromise.
Her crypt is full of flower-talk, and gladly
The stars come swimming down to kiss her face
Caught in its quiet splendor. Be still! Be still!
The place is full of angel-talk or song.

Here lies the fragile flower of Saint Francis
Stronger than armies! here, the unswerving gaze
Shuttered at last on earth, and turned on Godhead.

Here lies the testimony to Saint Francis:
Clare of Assisi.

                    Who weeps, weep but for joy.

ST. CLARE

WITNESS TO ST. CLARE: 20TH CENTURY

(St. Clare was proclaimed the patroness
of television by Pope Pius XII.)

Louder than jetplanes, soars her requiem
Unended till the ultimate bird records
On tapes of wind his final cadenced praise
Of dying Clare who thanked for having lived.

When all the bombs have barked their bitterness
Against creation, pocked earth's comeliness
With pitted rage, nature may yet remember
Clare found it ripe for singing, small to love.

Then go and blame her hostile bed of straw,
Refuse your absolution to her vigils,
My prophylactic world! But still be wary:
Her light may dim your calculating day;

And when you prove her penances archaic,
Render her life forever obsolete,
Clare may detour your space ships, rout your reason,
And lay her mantle on your television.

SONG
FOR A FRUSTRATE
ANCHORESS–
ST. COLETTE OF
CORBIE

(St. Colette, a Poor Clare of the 15th century,
was called from her anchorhold of prayer to
restore the primitive Rule of St. Clare where
it had lapsed into mediocrity or collapsed into ruin.)

Where is there anathema, I wonder,
Worthy for such a tragedy as made
The Lady Poverty dully shear her gleaming
Hair, and hush her singing? Who has lent
The dancing bride of Francis heavy feet?

If Clare in her beatitude is shaken,
Tasting the salt of mortal tears again,
Where shall we find a scourge to fit the makers
Of ruin? See the little nests all broken,
Swaying among the dark, foreboding trees.
And Poverty walks lonely with her lantern
Seeking a lover, weeping all in vain.

But while we talk of curses, search for scourges,
The gentle Clare is bargaining in bliss—
All the peace of Heaven sweetly troubled
With her insistence! Not so easily
Will Clare who broke the rocky wills of Pontiffs
Suffer erosion to find her beautiful dream!

So, sigh, my little anchoress, in your stronghold
Of quiet . . . it is frail, if Clare is strong!
Nor tears nor cries shall move her for your pity
Till God be bribed with her seraphic love
To seal your ears, Colette, to steal your seeing.

Meek Clare and fragile Francis make demands
On God with love that shakes the floors of Heaven,
With love that humbles stars, deflates the clouds,
And moves the Everlasting Arms to wrench you
Out of your lovely night, Colette, to day.

Yours be the holy curse of Clare and Francis:
Threat of the cruel road and talk and strife,
Yours be the always-going out of haven,
Yours be the terrible martyrdom of reclaim.

But if you buy back our dark in your harsh daylight,
Ransom our silence with your persistent pleas,
If you give back to Poverty her singing,
Rebuild the broken nests to the first pure folly,

After you drift to dust, exonerating
Your solitude, at last, poor anchoress,
Gone long-road-wandering, we shall call you, Mother
Forever. And Clare will claim you like a crown.

GENEALOGY

In those days, Francis smiled a revolution,
And all the rusted spearpoints of the Gospel
Shot on complacency. The world was wounded
Straight through its satisfaction. He begot
A generation of nomads set to wander
Across the earth like songs that drift to Heaven.

He had a daughter, Clare, who lost her heart
Entirely to a Lover Who solemnly promised
Her nothing on earth, and Paradise thereafter.

And she was barren, as the courteous sun
That lends its fire to moon and stars, reserving
Its burning glory whole, is brightly barren.
Barren as plainsong seeding the soul with hunger
For Heaven, barren as innocence of skies
That roof whole sinning worlds with vast compassion,
Barren by splendid vow, was the virgin Clare.

These are the children of her barrenness:
Singers who shatter the patient night's repose
With prayer like thunderclaps of poetry
And songs like sudden lilacs, cloistered deep
In niches of the cathedralled universe.

In their generations, who will number
The daughters of the barrenness of Clare,
Pouring their lives like smiling waters into
The world's dry riverbeds? Now, in the census
Of seven hundred years, write: She begot
Each of these virgins in these secret cloisters
And all who keep vigil beneath some layers of earth
For the glad final count. Let the virgin's daughters
Rise up and call her, Mother! Thanks be to God.

PSALM 151 – A PILGRIMAGE SONG

(After the drouth in the desertland,
      comes the saving rain.
Once it came to usher in the feast of St. Clare,
she who once routed armies with the Eucharistic Host
and received from Jesus the promise:
      "I will always take care of you.")

for the Choirmaster

I will show you a panorama of death and life ∗
Reduced to size of you, little ones and poor.
    I will buy back green lace for a shrunken tree ∗
    Brown with thirst, named all-unbeautiful.

for the chorus

Power of Yahweh less in thunder fells us ∗
Than in the green lace sudden on a tree
    Too small for anyone's work or attention ∗
    Save Father, Son, and Spirit laboring.

for the Choirmaster

I will peg down the corners of a sky *
Square over all your minim world I made
>*To tell in grey My Name you die to say* *
>*Except I toss the single cream of cloud /*
>*To let you see I know in vigiled grey*
The whiteness of your joy in radiant Clare *
Who Wheaten Disc held, and admonished Me.

for the chorus

Yahweh, with our bare toes here grass-nuzzling, *
As we spell out Compline under sky
>*Foaming Clare-symbol out of mysteried-grey,* *
>*We promise always to take care of You.*

for the Choirmaster

Lift up your heads, well veiled before my Presence, *
Take with My careful cameras of your eyes
>*Picture of three small apples on young crabtree,* *
>*Revelation of My love for you.*

for the chorus

Sing for parched tree unbeautiful come alive, *
Brave with small fern to fan earth's fears away!
>*Raise a glad shout for unmistakable portents* *
>*Murmurous with His hid and familiar Name.*
Dance! Dance! Dance! oh, dance, my sisters! *
Converted be to Yahweh who has made
>*Elfin apples to delight you, loves you,* *
>*Thinks you, dreams you! O Lord, alleluia!*

FRANCISCAN ROUNDELAY

"Your arrows / have put their point in me."
—Responsory, Feast of St. Francis

Your arrows have put
Their point in me:
My self is flowing out.
Out of the dark
Runs me to light,
To life. Ho!
In sudden brook runs me!

Hi! wide do I fling
Me east and west,
Spend me on south and north.
My heart's a point
Your arrows found
For pain. Ah!
Pierced now, I'm sudden free.

My dams of defense
Are stricken! Quick
And fatal speed Your darts.
Rushes the tide
To God-ed shore.
Your arrows
Have put their point in me!

IV.
LIFE, JOY,
PAIN

CONCERNING SOLITUDE

Down in this cave
Where sky itself is window
With lilac trees etched in its smooth blue panes,
There were to be, I thought, the two of us:
You on that cross, me listening at Your feet.

Why was the wasp invited? I must ask
You, for he was in no design of mine.

Whence this small devil's advocate
To threaten
Dear tenderness of silence with dark buzz,
Describing quick circumference of my head,
And monotoning: "Ho! you may be bitten!"?

He is a black suggestion to depart.
Silence is dangerous, "You may be bitten."
Perils are swirling in all cavey coolness
Of essence stripped of action down to being.

Listening to God is full of hazards.
Look what You came to, Christ on that wild tree!
I had better go; I might be bitten.
Work is waiting. Wasp, I hear you tell me.

I may be bitten,
Drone you on and on
Until I understand how necessary
You are, black wasp, when sky's so near for taking
And earth assumes small shape, is all contingent,
Is purely secondary.

Christ, oh! Lover,
Dead for me and for me risen, take
My small resolve:

I stay, forever listen,
Better for knowing
How I might be bitten.

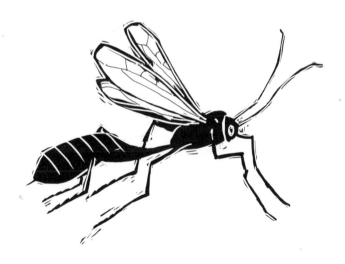

THE FEAST

"And which of you, if he ask his father
for bread, will he give him a stone?"
—Mt 7, 9-11

The cupped heart waits for bread,
And granite words
Are spread before its hunger.

Shall the teeth
Of sorrow bite the stone,
Or shall the tongue
Toll jeremiads on such stony feast?

Unwilling-slow, the cupped heart closes on
The petric fare
And finds the stone is bread.

REPLE CORDIS INTIMA

Slowly, leaving a path of smiles behind me,
I ventured my unspectacular escape
Off into hills staring with pitiful blindness
On my stripped grief. I went to tear my feet
On dear compassionate rocks out past the silence.

Cleverly the cave was clawed,
And cautiously, into the topmost hill's
Black bony side. Good, good to rip the hands
On such enduring work! So I
Moved in.

No one would find me, questions all come back
Marked: "Please return to the asker—
Insufficient address."

It was a safe cave, good for grieving,
Proofed against water, sound, and healing.
Well spent the skin's tear, eyes' burn, soul's deforming,
Until the Spirit wrecked with gentleness
(Not troubling to stake out claims for His occupation)
That heart's heart
Where Christ's fountainous tears keep falling.

PARABLE

Valiant and unafraid, the moss-rose judiths
Advanced against the cactus, closing in
With skirts of fluttering scarlet, gold, flecked-pink,
On formidable bared teeth of waiting thorn.

    This holofernes lapsed into no stupor
    Of spiney languor. Brutal and tall, he stood
    Proof (he thought) against all lovely moss-rose.

But then the judiths danced and took position
In absolute arabesques between his fangs
Of thorn, besieging him with gold and scarlet
Cries of love, too occupied with telling
Beauty's tale to fear death-freighted points.

    It was all too much for holofernes.
    Unkilling and unkilled, he took the moss-rose
    Under his tent of sudden-protective thorn.

And then he broke my heart. And all the judiths
Wept, to see the cactus show a rose.

QUEEN OF THE WORLD

Lady, your hard throne lurches
On our careening lives.

                        What sovereign sits
So perilous on exaltation, Mary,
As yours, borne on your children's gaucherie?

Call up to homage all the drooping fans
Of eyelashes, invite long-unbent knees
Down to obeisant dust before your slender
Security of love, queen!

                   "Queen!" a husky-throated
World will sing on faltering pitch forever
Because you dare to speed our sweating highways,
Ride our air pockets, swim our brine of tears.

Filigree lady, you outwear the leather
Of disillusion. You unsnarl despair
To hope's bright skein. No perilous exaltation
Is yours who sit in state our blundering.

LUMEN CORDIUM

A beam were merciful. A ray
Preserves in its piercing, pity,
Having limit and fences of dark. How many watts
Burn in Your daylamp, Spirit,
Picking out ravellings on the floor of the heart?

Flail the last shadow with light, and leave me
No littlest lovely shade for sweet concealings.
Filter the very palms against my face,
Let up the blinds of eyelids.

If I defy You,
Sun, with a final and favorite shadow, play me
False with Your highest voltage. Put Your pity's
Garments by, and smite me with Your Light.

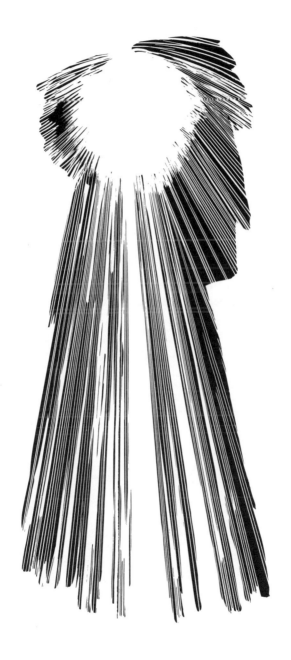

TWO FESTIVALS

I.

It needed the boldness of humility
To face the yellow day and know
Its light came out of the fire, fire
In me, and sun was mere moon-mirror
Of my heart. Better not tell them, either,

How I did not play the organ, only
Looked at the cream and black of it and said:
Fiat! and it was done; how out of me
The music obediently waterfalled as I
Listened, not much amazed,
Having housed this heart a long time now.

The day smelled of my spices. Oh, yes,
I knew they were God's, but then
Faith is taking Him for granted.
And I have seen well enough God's beautiful mirth
When I strew myself around the day and
The universe, and hills clap hot applause
For Him, for His beautiful mirth.

II.

There had to be an invocation now:
Come, sunlight, seek, soak, saturate
Hinges of me. Make havoc of my neatly
Persistent pain. I push against my doors
That will not fling, and am rewarded with
A crack of gold light, just enough to warm me
Into walking, smiling, and deceiving.

God, give music to this crate before me!
In mercy blunt the weariness that nibbles
My spine with delicate teeth. I think that never
I heard a song. And how does music feel
Under the fingers? I cannot recall.

I only remember faith means always
Taking Him for granted:
Grace so sure, so fleet on perilous scaffold
Of my spine;
Mystery of God's mirth looks out
From cages of my fingers.
Grind your poor spice down, loved God.
The while my heart goes shouting: Festival!

EXORCISM FOR SADNESS

Lift off my shoulders, you
Black, caressing, insistent wings!
Depart out of my mind's deep cavern, you
Settlers with all your gibbering reminders
Of winds' kiss, bright skies' cherishing.

Go, go plunge down love's last
Little hill of summer, into the sea
That burns with all your kind, salt
On the soul's poor rawness, threat
To the watched eyes each new terrible
Moment.

By hope I command you,
Lash you out with faith gone fierce
In final stand and final fall, last groping.
Back now! back to your hell. Down, down!

EXAMINATION OF CONSCIENCE

I hiss at the uncomely cat
To go and leave me Sunday in this grass.
(How did the creature slip past his Creator
Without receiving dowry of that grace
To cats peculiar?) So unfortunate,
He bears his low-slung self on awkward legs
Ridiculously thick.

      The clipped coat is
Unstrokable black cotton. Stricken calls
Of everlasting hunger are his song.

There on the piered enclosure gates he sprawls,
Mimicking the lions of St. Mark's,
Crying that I admire him, fetch him milk,
Sure I find him fetching as a kitten.

I hiss again. I'll not resort to hose
(It's out of reach), but fiercely clap my hands
In sharp dismissal which he thinks applause
And pays me with two clownish leaps.

       Oh, that
Slack string of tail! Cat, help me to forgive
Meows that swear me better than I am!

ON STEWARDSHIP

"You may keep it forever," the child said.

With lovely thievery, she took my shell
From out my pond,
And tendered it to me.

Where shall I snatch an elegance to match
The moment, robe me right for the occasion?
Or how not stand bewildered, sudden shabby,
Before the child's grave judgement on my worth?

Tried by her unfathomable juried—
Thought, I hear my sentence handed down,
And owner once, am sudden steward now.
"You may keep it forever," she decrees.

Unburdened now of holdings, I go, glad
To do her bidding, understanding how
The earth no less than heaven
Is a child's.

V.
CHRIST
THE LORD

ANNUNCIATION

Swifter than jet-cleaved air is ribboned, love flies
By flawless automatics of the heart
Back to this hour, girl, and angel, curving
Wings of its own against her lifted face.

Here is the home of hours and of ages
Toward which time groped, and flowing eternities.
Ever will love return and close this hour
Warm on its starkest cry and brightest song.

Haven and hangar built by God for hostel
On the macadam bleakness of whatever
Threatens or comes, love praises best this hour
With petals of silence strewn along its lintel.

ADVENT SONG

Season of tempest and magnificence
Is mercy for the heart. We bear the thunder
Standing, but this hush upon the heart,
This hour of low kindling of the stars,
This snowflake silence of your coming, Child,
Anvils our shapely words back into dumbness.

The Lord is near! He leaves no space for crouching
Safe against His gaze. The dimes and nickles
Of our falseness hit on gleaming pavements
Of His coming, for the Lord is near

As songs we have not sung yet, Love is lurking
In nebulae of breath, is perched on spiral
Of rib, swims arteried lakes, is coming, coming!

Might is a concept any slave can live by.
Churls with bent necks confess Omnipotence;
But help us, Child, to walk this wild, sweet country
Of hush and waiting. Teach us how to yearn.

ADVENT PROPHECY

Where tortured atoms writhe beneath the scalpel
Of our investigations, I see her coming,
Branches of flowering pity in her arms,
Healing the day with glances. And the atoms
Fall down to kiss her feet, and are made whole.

I hear the clash of prophecies converging
On the faint stir of Life beneath her heart.
Down our loud boulevards, I see her coming.
Lift up your heads! Blow all your factory whistles!
And point the hour on your telechrons!

Not to Ain Karim. To the laboratories
Where astronauts sit trim in new space jackets,
I see her coming, space held in one hand;
Her smile forgiving all the bright moon-rockets
Their errors, with the moon beneath her feet.

Girl of Isaias' vision, could he see you
Carry your Son into our plastic jungles
And cure our tuneless music with your singing?
Hour Isaias never dreamed is striking:
Under the neon lights, I see her coming!

Lift up your heads! You tall TV antennae,
Lean down and prostrate for her coming! Jet planes,
Hum the glad antiphons of our redemption!
Once over hills, now through the chromium maze,
The young girl light with Child shall come and save us.

VENI, DATOR MUNERUM

Those were small signs, those burning tongues.
What acts of what apostles shall set down
For sober students of that hour to read
The blue-white spurtings off those rivetted hearts?

Wind told the fateful Coming, or Wind was
Itself the Comer, Coming, the Arrived.
Let no nice speculations crowd what moment
Old walls of souls go down, thoughts gale away
Out of safe reason, logic's house has not
Stone on a stone, and men are immediate martyrs.

Swiftly the Gift is given with secret fire
Still, in this slipping twilight. The almost-night
Knows the Wind coming. Giver with gifts, He comes
Surely, at timidest call, at hand's most feeble
Beckoning from the sucking sands.

Oh, Giver!
I guess what fatal gifts you bring me! Give me
Some gift to bear Your gifts. Your consolation
Has blown me from the branches of my comforts.

OUR LADY OF THE ASCENSION

Fold your love like hands around the moment.
Keep it for conference with your heart, that exit
Caught on clocks, by dutiful scribes recorded
Less truly than in archives of your soul.

Turn back from His going, be His still-remaining.
Lift the familiar latch on cottage door . . .
Discover His voice in corners, hear His footfalls
Run down the porches of your thoughts. No powers

However hoarse with joy, no Dominations
Curved with adoration guess what whispers
Of: "Mother, look!" and "Mother, hurry!"
Glance off the cottage walls in shafts of glory.

How shall your heart keep swinging longer, Mary?
Quickly, quickly, take the sturdy needle
Before your soul crowds through your flesh! the needle
And stout black thread will save you. Take the sandal

Peter left for mending. After that,
The time is short, with bread to bake for John.

PENTECOST: FIRST VESPERS

Come upon us, walking
Toward You feeding
There among the lilies
In fabulous no-karat gilt
Vases.

To that old one who maintains a balance
Precariously nice, and to that young one
Whose walk is rushing wind and flailing arms, come,
Spirit! be alerted at the sound
Of bare feet speaking to You on bare board.

Into these tender moments while we wait
The great bells gone subpoena-ing the air
To bear You to us, Wind and Fire and Light
In vesperal magnificence, come, slip
Through the low portals of our hearts instead,
Guest too familial for appointed hour,
Lover too loved to need formal attire.

Come to us, kneeling,
And our arms stretched
Wide and up, waiting Your embrace.
See the dowry that we bring You, Lover:
Each her unholiness, each her ache of need.

This is the little court of love, this motley
Assortment of us, Spirit, loving You
Together, and together miracled
Into the splendor of community.

Come upon us, Love of God. Come on us,
Spirit of truth unravelling mystery
Lightly as alleluias on your poor ones,
Your holy community,
My loved company.

FESTIVALE: TWO MOVEMENTS

for Our Lady's Assumption

I. *When stars fall back in wonder, and the sun*
    Shields his golden eye against such fire
    As Mary is, returning to her Son,

    What bourdon stops of sea-roar underscore
    The lightning's corno, while the morning chimes
    Against the noon, the night, the evermore!

II. *But there is pianissimo for heart,*
    And love is dulcet where the flowers stand
    In open-petalled wonder at her tomb.

    Call back the flutes and violins of spring!
    And find them still too clangorous for love
    Singing its silence at her empty grave.

THE KINGDOM

Sky taut above, across, beyond
Candor of plain and arrogance of mountain
Is not, after all, surprising,
No more than tension of earth turned precisely
Right, is.
We may expect exactitude of God.

Smaller details of local administration
May be, admittedly, endearing.
Only churls will fail to credit
Contriving of flowers
On planets' sweating faces.

Even the notion of cornered stars
To prick light-holes in night
Is quaintly charming:
God indulging His fancies.

If He sometimes ripples the land with breezes,
We can be clever to recognize His mirth
Over our shredding atoms, pestering space
With rocket inquiries.
God is patient with children.

All is predictable, given Him:
Throb of a thousand worlds in ordered traffic,
Persistence of birds against the longest war.
We can depend on God to stoke the fires
Of sun each day and quarter the years
With seasons.

Only, who will explain His crown,
Spiney?

COMMUNITY CONCERTO FOR CHRIST THE KING

First Movement:

> *The violin snapped a string.*
> *Bow, warped, went some astray*
> *On measure well intended.*

Second Movement:

> *Piano. No, it cannot be*
> *Quite tuned. It is too old.*
> *Hear that tonal descent?*

> *Now has it tolled*
> *Disaster for conductor?*
> *No, see His own*
> *Sure-held baton rubs wound*
> *In hand by nail rent.*

Finale:

> *So was this whole assembly:*
> *Bent, broken, and disabled*
> *For all symphonic roll*

> *Save they were led*
> *By strangest of conductors . . .*
> *King, He looked*
> *On podium of cross there, and evoking*
> *Impossible beauty.*
> *In His hand, a nail hole.*

THE LIGHT OF HIS FACE

"It was your strength . . . and the
light of your Face that saved them."
—psalm 44

Canto I: Bethlehem

The light of His face was scarcely
Something to blind,
To silence, to smite the heart
Down by His power. It was, after all,
A child's face only,
Had irregular paths
Of tears traced on the cheeks,
Had lips that trembled
In the cold.

Yet kings found strength to go
Back another way, post-adoration,
Fearless of Herod, careless of all that was
Except the face, the light of the face
Of the Child.

Shepherds before had come and known the light
As homely and good, face with an infant's smile
Arched for the joy of shepherds' pipes, and liking
Dancing within the cave.

                    It was the light,
The light of the face that spun them back to hillsides
No longer dark, blazed bright with angels' singing
Knocking off ridges, echoing down the slant
Of sheep on sided hills, shepherds glorifying,
Praising, praising strong, the light of the face.

There was no longer another task to do.

Canto II: The Temple

Waiting and fasting, fasting and waiting.
Came in the years, and years went out again
For Anna and Simeon bending weak on stick
Of prophecy bone-slender, till that day

When strength came, no! not striding, riding rather
In chariot of arms, and face turned on
The cooing doves in wonder at the things
A bird can show a child, how to propel
On wing the little cage-space of a world
For one thing.

             On some later day a man
Would tell the marvel that no sparrow falls
To earth except the Father's face record
In light that little life-span. Would He, too,
The man, think back to pigeons for king's ransom?
No matter.

             Here the two, the vigilant fasters,
Stand sudden straight before the small face turned
Away from twittering birds to them, oh! them!

Comes canticle! The prophecy girds on sinew
There in the light of the face of the ransomed Child,

Proclaims that light revealing to all nations
The glory of His people Israel.

Canto III: Egypt

Under the hood of blanket was the light,
Light of the face of helpless fugitive
Giving somehow, some way, strength to the man
Hard striding by the mule, and the mule not needing
Goad or persuasion either, having seen
Likewise itself the light of the face that leaned
Against the breast of the girl.

                        The burro trotted,
Sudden Arabian steed, in the light of the face
That made of the girl an army set in array
To defend the Child, to armor Him with kisses.

Somehow the burro knew, the man had ken,
The girl understood their strength came out
From the light of the face of the Child
That they could save Him.

Canto IV: The Temple's Doctors

Never the brushed beards more relentlessly stroked
By fingers set to ease minds' need for leaping
Up from consideration to conclusion. Stopping
Never a moment, fingers tell the secret:

Light has swung in on long, dark pondering.
Light from the face, the face of the questioning Boy.

Who could bear answers, sort them, rout them, parry
Answer with answer, only can smitten sit
Before the questions, before the light of the face
Of the young questor.

Already the Savior saves
With questions, and forever. Will you also
Go away? And: woman, who accused you?
What did you speak of on the way? Whom do you
Say that I am? What have I done? Whom seek you?

Thread your beards, doctors, with your quickened fingers
Against a someday question: Do you love Me,
Love me more than these? It will need strong
Light to fell a heart down to confess it:

In all things knowing, Lord, this, too, you know.

Canto V: Cana of Galilee

Shake them, the tambourines! Let lutes be tuned
Up to bridalissimo! Bring wine
To quicken dancers' feet.

                      Here was rehearsal
For sitting down to banquet with the Father
One day in Heaven. Here of Galilee
In Cana was a wedding, and was Jesus
Prophesying Heaven with His handclasp,
His blessing on men's feasting, oh! His laughter!

No one said it. Enough that all there knew it:
How strength to plumb the mystery of feasting
Aright came from the light of the Rabbi's face.

It was the light of His face spotlighted dancing
Out of stumble's danger, pitched the singing
Pure and sweet, reflected on the bride's cheeks
Pink of innocent dawn, and summoned water
Into roseate wine.

                    And all there learned it.
It was His mother knew it from recall.

There was a wedding in Cana,
And the Mother of Jesus was there.

Canto VI: Calvary

The light of His face was scarcely
Something to blind,
To silence, to smite the heart
Down by His power. It was, after all,
A spent face only,
Had irregular paths
Of tears traced on the cheeks,
Had lips that would not
Curse the day.

Yet, prostitute found power
To take a Cross-stand, testify her love
Stronger than jeering soldiers who remembered
Other days and her, nights in the town.
Fearless of lewd jibes, careless of all that was
Except the light of the bleeding face
On the Cross,

Magdalene, bereft of seven devils
Stood with the sinless Mother of Jesus' face.

To keep Him further company, there was
A thief, suspending shrewdness of his trade
For wisdom's favor, sudden strike on heart's
Eye long-crusted from the light, now letting
Up protesting eyelid on a day

Not dreamed of. Sudden heir to Paradise,
A thief found his long-looted essence, cried out
In ecstasy of faith from cross to Cross,
To sunset face of Christ, Remember me!

Canto VII: The Kingdom

We give you thanks, O God most kind, devising
Apocalypse to suit our piteous need.

For milk-white steeds, for angels with gold censers,
For elders bent, for each of the forty-four thousand,
Be praised, kind God!

*   Till strength is gathered from*
Your face that our face can behold forever
Your unveiled Face.

*   This canto goes unfinished.*

VI.
END OF
THE DAY

PSALM FOR THE MOTHER OF GOD

Sleeved and skirted in sun, informed with Spirit,
Invade the moments of my history,
Mary, with all your terrible bright battalions.

You are less cadence than sinew of my songs,
Girl whose smiles run down my joys, O woman
Whose fiat! *blames my sleep of sorrow. Mary,*

Loop my feet retreating with your glances,
Ropes of lilacs stouter than any chain!
Virgin of perspective, focus me

Fast on your Son, and catch my straying glances,
Little foxes, in your trap of hands.
Less cadence be than sinew of my songs.

MEDITATION ON DEATH

Your eyes have split the atoms of my desires
Until my bones curve into cadences,
My blood swirls into songs.

Who shall penetrate my outer spaces,
Investigate the mystery of my being?
Tell me on what eternal holiday

Your Love traced out my avenues, hands made
Crannies and crooks for pain, hills for delight?
O spread, clear map of me on lap of God!

Now shall I praise You for the sheltering skull
Around my thoughts that tune my low Te Deum
When Your eyes split the atoms of my desires.

TOURIST

(for Sister Madeleva on All Saints' Day, 1964)

It was the grand conducted tour,
Down boulevards of psalms,
Along the winding-pathed responsories
Looking back upon themselves
With quaint design and canny emphasis.
God was the guide. Divine enthusiasm
Is something, I find, to throw the heart offguard.

So I forgot to check itinerary,
Let Him go His wildly wonderful way,
Love careening through a mass of heroes,
Treading down saints in winey victory.

I saw the slain Lamb reigning, heard God praise
His Mother for believing, saw St. John
Crowned with his head by angels.
Then God said,
My saints! One steps back into doorwayed awe
Seeing God moved like this. One looks away.

Apostles draining chalices, young girls
Dancing with lamps that spill love on the floors
Of Heaven, and a thousand thousand men
With girt loins, fingers curled eternally
Around a staff of bliss,—I saw them all.
It was, I say, the grand conducted tour.

Only when I ran between the peals
Of glory, looked for rest from majesty
Too thick, too heady for my long enduring,
Sat panting on a low stump south of Heaven,
Did I discover you, sweet lady, singing
A small and secret song, the little stars
Of your bright earthly lauding massed about you,
Flowers nuzzling at your ankles, wonder
Caught forever and ever on your face.

MIDNIGHT OFFICE: FEAST OF THE HOLY TRINITY

Fingers against light switches, together, we tore
Some little yellow holes out of the dark,
Enough to read incredibilities
Out of our neat black books.

Somewhere a train
Bellowed its lonely protest at the night,
And homeless winds cursed all our adamant walls.
Sleep was not routed, only subdued, still scratching
Its claims at eyelids, urging its right against
Scaffold of spine put up on fantastic hour,
When incense took the air into its arms
And kissed it sweet, when clear command rang out:
Come and adore, true One in Three
And Three not falsed in One!

Crazily, moths swung into the yellow holes
Punched in the night, but voices kept insisting:
True God in Trinity One! Come, and adore Him.

Not only where vigilant choirs sing: Holy, holy,
Holy forevermore, outside our cages
Of dwindling days and space, of vanishing faces,
Shall God be told His Name.

The secret rings
Here, against brick, on board, invests the night
With wildest glory, unhinges the universe
From time, as stunned from sleep these nuns bow heads,
Bend shoulders, tune the throats still flaked with silence
Crying: O Beata Trinitas!

COMPLINE: RESPONSORY

*Faith is for the morning
When all things wait to be revealed.
Love is the name of noontide
Striking fullness of the day.
But hope belongs to nightfall
When everything is done.

Lord, let me venture on the day
With faith that waits for sure delight
Somehow, some moment to appear
And make deific sense of all that is.

*Faith is for the morning
When all things wait to be revealed.

Break me Your strength to sweat at noon
When love's a fire I will not flee
For cooler places and remote
That never knew a spendthrift's glee.

**Love is the name of noontide
Striking fullness of the day.

But at the nightfall when the dark
Exclaims in stars that light is far
Past reach of realness, make blindfold
Upon my heart the dearest thing I own.

**But hope belongs to nightfall
When everything is done.

*Faith is for the morning
When all things wait to be revealed
And Glory be to Father is the tune.
Love is the name of noontide
Striking fullness of the day
With Glory be to Son in victory.
But hope belongs to nightfall
When everything is done
And only Glory be to Spirit is.

ORGAN VOLUNTARY

(Suitable for weddings, jubilees, funerals)

Begin with pianissimo. Accent
The unlost chord
That each day keeps on finding
Least lost when lowest sung.

Bring in the pedal:
Sustain the note that first unslung my stars
And tilts them yet with very wonderment.

You have to understand a fugue goes on
Forever,
Not arriving, only seeking
The single theme it speaks
In variations.

It leads, and you must follow where it climbs
To climax and falls back to start again
A new ascent. (Sustain the pedal, please.)

Bring in the strings, the winds,
And let them say
What way He went and comes
And is forever
Fugue of my life
And final decrescendo.

STRANGE GODS BEFORE ME — Mother Mary Francis

In this book Mother Mary Francis writes, "A number of strange little gods have established themselves on high pedestals in our generation. There is the convex god who pushes the world away, a top-heavy god who demands worship of tragic proportions, a surface god who will not tolerate his clients looking into the deeps of life, a neurotic god whose converts are legion in our day, and a few others. It is quite possible for worshippers of the true God to fall under the spell of these idols. Their doctrines are glossy. They have the new look. And they create an environment. In fact, this is their peculiar office."

This is a series of reflections on the many attachments that impede our attempts to relate to the true God. All kinds of preoccupations that fill man's time and often interfere with his true purpose in life. All who read this book will discover some personal applications that will help sweep away so many obstacles in our search for God.